DATA MIGRATION COCKPIT IN SAP S/4HANA CLOUD

*A Step-by-Step Guide to Using
the Data Migration Cockpit in S/4HANA
Cloud with Use Cases for Finance Objects*

AMRISH MOHAN, CPA

TABLE OF CONTENTS

1. INTRODUCTION

In writing this guide, I have attempted to provide you with practical information on the data migration process using the *Data Migration Cockpit* app in S/4HANA Cloud. I have made every effort to explain the features and capabilities in a specific and easy to understand manner and avoid technical jargon and marketing statements.

Within S/4HANA Cloud, the *Data Migration Cockpit* app is the only SAP tool available for performing data migrations. SAP has streamlined the data migration process in S/4HANA Cloud, making it intuitive and user-friendly thereby giving a lot of control to functional team members and a tech savvy business user over the migration process. I have successfully performed data migrations on multiple S/4HANA Cloud projects without needing a technical resource.

While this guide is specifically written for S/4HANA Cloud, this guide can be followed for S/4HANA On-Prem edition as well.

I hope you find this guide useful.

2. SAP S/4HANA Cloud – An Overview

SAP S/4HANA Cloud is a future-ready Enterprise Resource Planning (ERP) system with built-in intelligent technologies, including AI, machine learning, and advanced analytics. It helps transform business processes with intelligent automation, is built for the cloud, and runs on SAP HANA – a market-leading in-memory database that offers real-time processing speeds and a dramatically simplified data model.

Source: SAP.com

S/4HANA Cloud is a Software-as-a-Service (SaaS) offering by SAP that runs on its in-memory HANA database. It provides a lot of capabilities for the core SAP ERP (Enterprise Resource Planning) offering, which SAP is known for, in cloud.

You can visit www.SAP.com for more information on the S/4HANA Cloud product and its capabilities and use cases.

3. Data Migration Cockpit in S/4HANA Cloud

3.1 OVERVIEW

Data migration in simple terms is the process of identifying, extracting, transforming, and loading data from the source system into the target system. Successful data migration delivers high-quality, error-free data thereby enabling the underlying business processes. Performing successful data migration is and always will be one of the key requirements/ deliverables of any SAP implementation.

3.2 MIGRATION COCKPIT

With S/4HANA Cloud, SAP delivers a robust, user-friendly tool in the form of *Data Migration Cockpit* for performing data migrations. The data migration cockpit app as shown in Figure 3.2.A supports migrating data from SAP and non-SAP systems into S/4HANA Cloud. It comes pre-delivered with over 150 plus objects across various process areas. We will be covering some of the objects delivered within the financial process in a later chapter.

The data migration cockpit has been delivered under Scope ID BH5. Please refer to the link below for the SAP documentation on BH5 scope ID. https://rapid.sap.com/bp/scopeitems/BH5

Figure 3.2.A: Data Migration Cockpit Fiori app.

Here are some of the key features of the *Data Migration Cockpit* app:

» Delivered Out-of-the Box

The data migration cockpit is delivered and ready to use and needs no special configuration or setup. To use the app, relevant security roles need to be assigned to appropriate users. Please refer to the **Security Roles** section for role details.

» No Additional Licensing

The data migration cockpit is included as part of the standard S/4HANA Cloud subscription. No additional licensing or fees are required.

» SAP Recommended Approach

The *Data Migration Cockpit* is the only SAP tool available for performing migrations in the S/4HANA Cloud system. It is also the recommended approach for migrating data from SAP and non-SAP systems into S/4HANA Cloud.

» Simulation & Monitoring

Within the migration cockpit, we can simulate and monitor the data before migrating it to S/4HANA Cloud. This provides an opportunity to validate and correct any errors before the data is loaded. We will cover this topic in more detail in the next section.

» Perform Audits

Using the audit feature, we get the ability to assign random imported records for auditing.

» Ease of Use

This tool is very intuitive and easy to use. It can be used by functional and business team members with no development skills needed. The app provides for a state-of-the-art user experience with the Fiori UI and a faster response time.

» Parallel Processing

Multiple objects can be loaded simultaneously, allowing for a shorter migration timeline.

3.3 MIGRATION PROCESS

The migration process using the Data Migration Cockpit App can be broadly broken down into 9 steps as shown below. Some of these steps need to be performed only once while the rest need to be performed every time a migration is performed.

1. Setup Migration Project in S/4HANA Cloud
2. Activate migration object(s)
3. Download template(s)

4. Populate template(s)
5. Upload template(s)
6. Prepare staging tables
7. Perform Mapping Tasks
8. Perform Simulation
9. Migrate data

1. Setup Migration Project in S/4HANA Cloud

The first step in performing a data migration in S/4HANA Cloud is to set up a Migration Project. The Migration Project controls the migration process and monitoring of the objects that are being migrated. Setting up a Migration Project is typically a one-time activity. Once a Project or Project is created, they are used through the implementation.

You can set up a single Migration Project and perform all the migrations within it or set up multiple Migration Projects. Objects can be migrated simultaneously under multiple Migration Projects; however, the same object cannot be migrated simultaneously under two different Projects. The example below should help explain this feature.

Migration Project	Migration Object	Simultaneous Processing	Reason
Project A	Cost Center	Yes	Staging tables are different from Open Sales Order
Project B	Open Sales Orders	Yes	Staging tables are different from Cost Center
Project B	Cost Center	No	Cost Center cannot be migrated using Project B since the staging tables for cost center objects are locked under Project A. Once the cost center migration under Project A is complete, then the staging tables for the cost center are un-locked and additional cost center records can be migrated under Project B.

Tip: Set up Migration Projects by process areas. Example: A Migration Project to convert finance master data (cost centers, profit centers, GL balances, etc.,) and a separate Migration Project to convert Sales data (customers, open sales orders, sales contracts etc.,).

We will review the Migration Project and steps to create them in more detail under the section **Migration Cockpit Components.**

2. Activate migration object(s)

Once the Migration Project is set up, the next step is to add the relevant objects within the Migration Project. By adding objects within the Project, we enable them for migration. This is a one-time activity per Project.

Adding Objects in the Migration Project

From the Migration Project screen, click on **Settings**, then **Edit** and search for the object. Once the object has been found, click on **Used in project** as shown in Figure 3.3.A.

Within the **Predecessor Objects** column, the system displays a list of any dependent objects. From the **Documentation** column, we can access the SAP documentation for the objects.

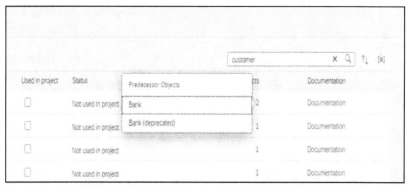

Figure 3.3.A: Migration objects selection screen.

Note: *You can find the list of migration objects at the link below:* http://help.sap.com/S4_CE_MO

3. Download template(s)

In this step, download the migration template file for the selected object. The template file is in XML format and can be used in Microsoft Excel. It contains instructions, a list of fields, and the actual template to populate.

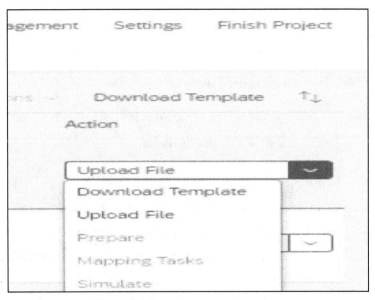

Figure 3.3.B: Project Migration screen.

Migration Templates

The migration template files include the following sheets:

» Introduction: Provides introduction to using templates in S/4HANA systems.

» Field List: Provides a list of fields available within that template and specifies if the fields are mandatory or optional, field lengths and type.

» Object Template sheets: These are the sheets where upload data needs to be populated. Based upon the migration objective, there could be one or more sheets. These are typically colored in Orange (required) and Blue (optional).

Template Size Limitations

Please be aware that the default size limit for each uploaded XML file is 100MB in S/4HANA Cloud.

4. Populate template(s)

The next step is to populate the template with the uploaded data. A few things to keep in mind at this step include:

» Do not hide, rename, or delete sheets within the template.
» Do not hide, rename, or delete columns within the template.
» Do not change the formatting of the cells or use formulas.
» Review the guidelines provided in the sheet titled **Introduction** within the template.
» Review the **Field List** sheet within the template to familiarize yourself with the required versus optional fields and field lengths to appropriately populate data.

Tip: You do not need to delete the **Introduction and Field List** sheets before uploading the data.

5. Upload template(s)

In this step, you upload the populated template into the Migration Cockpit. Once the template is uploaded, you will get the message *Data Successfully Transferred to Staging Tables* as shown in Figure 3.3.C.

You can click on *Show Messages* to avoid errors in reviewing and correcting the file.

Figure 3.3.C: Project Migration template upload screen.

6. Prepare staging tables

The next step in the process is to prepare the staging tables for the object to be migrated. You can do this by selecting the **Prepare** option from the **Action** column as shown in Figure 3.3.D. This step needs to be performed every time a file is being uploaded.

Depending upon the object being migrated, there could be more than one staging table. You can view the staging table list by clicking on **Tables** under the **Data** column or from the *Object Details* screen.

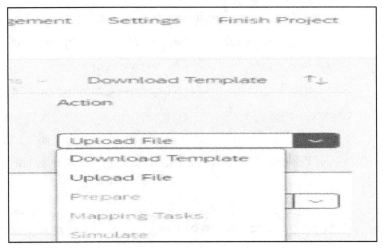

Figure 3.3.D: Project Migration screen.

Once the preparation has started, SAP sets the Object status to *Preparation Started* under the Migration Object column. You can view the status of this activity by clicking on **Running Activities** at the top of the screen. Errors can be viewed by clicking **on the Activities with Error** link.

7. Perform Mapping Tasks

In this step, we map and confirm the values from our template to the target system (S/4HANA Cloud) values. There are three types of mappings namely,

> » Fixed Mapping: You map the template field value to the default target field value. Example: Mapping *Controlling Area* field value to *A000*. In S/4HANA Cloud, you can only have one controlling area - A000.
> » Value Mapping: You map the template field value to the corresponding target field values. Example: Mapping cost center field.
> » Control Parameter: Specific fields within S/4HANA accept control parameter values. These values are configured within the system. Example: Field *Digital payment token* is a control parameter field. This field is part of the Customer master object.

You can check the status and type of the object mapping by clicking on the **Mapping Tasks** column within the Migration Project as shown in Figure 3.3.E.

Note: All mapping tasks need to be confirmed before you can proceed to the Simulation stage.

Figure 3.3.E: Project Migration mapping screen.

Another way to confirm the mappings is by downloading the mapping templates from the **Mapping Tasks** screen and populating the template and uploading them. You will still need to confirm the values to move to the Simulation stage.

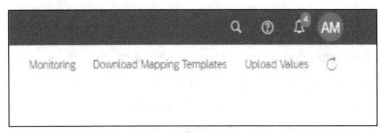

Figure 3.3.E: Project Migration mapping screen.

8. Perform Simulation

Once all the mapping tasks are confirmed, the next step is to simulate the transfer of data in the S/4HANA Cloud system. To perform this activity, select *Simulate* from the Action list as shown in Figure 3.3.F for the object being migrated.

Figure 3.3.F: Project Migration screen.

Note: *During the simulation stage, data is not written into the S/4HANA Cloud system. The purpose of this activity is to review the errors that would've occurred during an actual migration.*

Once the simulation has started, SAP sets the Object status to Simulation Started under the Migration Object column. You can monitor the status of the simulation activity from the Monitoring link at the top of the Migration Project screen.

Simulation Results

You can view the simulation results for the migration object under the *Simulation* column on the Migration Project screen as shown in Figure 3.3.F.

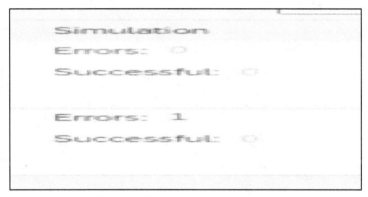

Figure 3.3.F: Project Migration screen.

You can click on the error count to view the error details as shown in Figure 3.3.G.

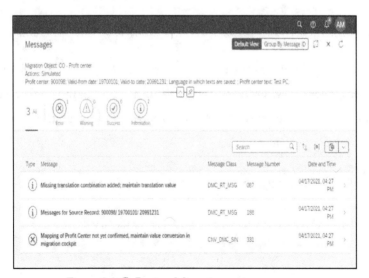

Figure 3.3.G: Project Migration messages screen.

9. Migrate data

This is the final step of the migration process. Once the simulation result is successful, you are ready to load your data into the S/4HANA Cloud system. To perform this activity, select *Migrate* from the Action list as shown in Figure 3.3.H. for the object being migrated.

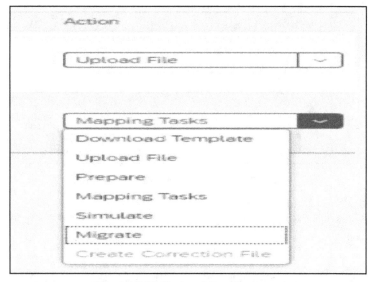

Figure 3.3.H: Project Migration screen.

Once the migration has started, SAP sets the Object status to *Migration Started* under the Migration Object column. You can monitor the status of the migration activity from the *Monitoring* link at the top of the Migration Project screen.

Note: Once the migration has started, it cannot be undone.

Migration Results

You can view the simulation results for the migration object under the *Migration* column on the Migration Project screen as shown in Figure 3.3.1.

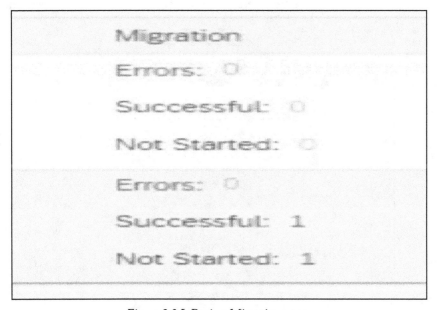

Figure 3.3.1: Project Migration screen.

Once the above steps are completed, the migration process is complete. The migrated data is now ready to be validated by the project team and subsequently by the business team.

Create Correction Files

In case of errors during the migration, you can create correction files which contain a list of all the records that have errors in the staging table. The records will need to be adjusted to ensure that errors are resolved and subsequently uploaded by following steps three through nine.

Monitoring Status

Using Data Migration Status, you can monitor the progress of the migration and view statistics for individual objects. Extended statistics are enabled by default. To disable the extended statistics, select Set Extended Statistics and set the status to OFF.

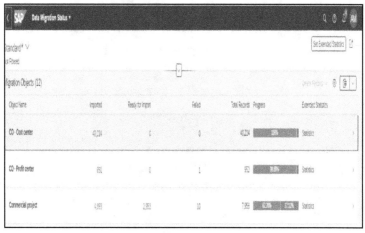

Figure 3.3.J: Data Migration Status screen

Auditing

The *Data Migration Status* app allows you to select records to perform the audit. To perform an audit of a migrated object, select the object and choose **Mass Assign Records for Audit** as shown in Figure 3.3.K. and specify the records for the audit as shown in Figure 3.3.L.

Figure 3.3.K: Object details screen.

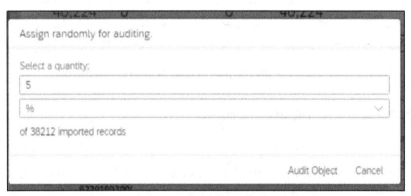

Figure 3.3.L: Assign records to the audit popup.

Once the audit review is complete, you can go back and set the **Audit Status** to Approved or Rejected.

3.4 MIGRATION COCKPIT COMPONENTS

Now that we have reviewed the key features and the migration process, let's look at the two main components of the migration cockpit. The two main components of the migration cockpit are:

1. Migration Project
2. Migration Object

Migration Project

In S/4HANA Cloud, a migration project is used to control and monitor all the activities related to data migration. The migration project is the first thing that needs to be set up within the *Data Migration Cockpit* app so that it can perform migration for any object. In essence, all migrations happen under a migration project. You can create and work with more than one migration project simultaneously within the system. Let's look at the migration project in a little more detail.

Setting up a migration project

To set up a migration project, you can access the *Data Migration Cockpit* app and click on the **Create** link. This will bring up the project creation screen as shown in Figure 3.4.A. On this screen, specify the **Project Name** and **Database Connection type.** By default, the Local SAP S/4HANA Database Schema is selected. **Mass Transfer ID** is a sequential number that gets generated and assigned for each migration project.

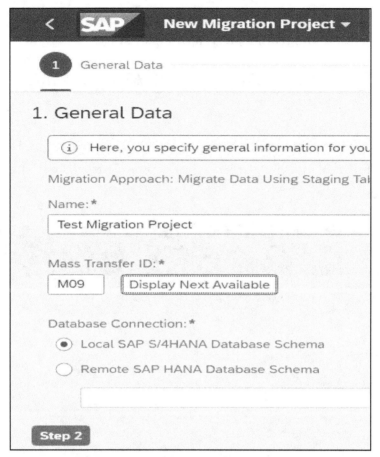

Figure 3.4.A: Project Migration creation screen.

Database Connection Types:

» Local S/4HANA Database: In this case, the staging tables are generated within the internal schema of the SAP S/4HANA Cloud system. This option is used when you want to migrate data only via the XML templates provided by SAP.

» Remote SAP HANA Database: In this case, the staging tables are generated in the schema of the remote SAP HANA database. This option is used when you want to migrate data via your own tools, ETL is an example of this.

Note: *In both types of connections, the data is transferred to staging tables.*

Figure 3.4.B. shows a migration project titled **Test Migration Project.** Upon clicking on the project, we see the project details as shown in Figure 3.4.C.

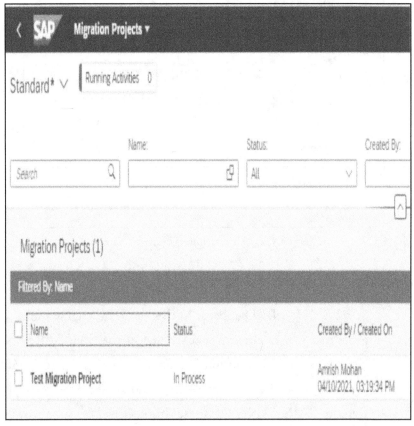

Figure 3.4.B: Migration projects screen.

Figure 3.4.C: Project Migration detail screen.

Migration Project Screen Details

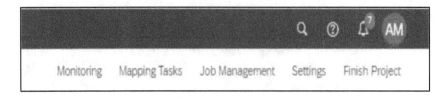

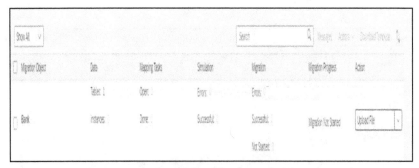

Figure 3.4.C1: Project Migration detail screen.

The project migration detail screen contains the following:

1. Monitoring: This allows you to monitor the status of all activities executed within the project migration. You can filter the results based on object (example: cost center), action (example: preparation), Status (example: completed/failures), user, and date as shown in Figure 3.4.D.

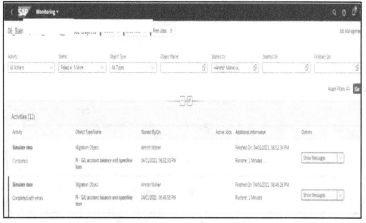

Figure 3.4.D: Project Migration monitoring details.

2. Mapping Tasks: This displays a list of all the mapping tasks for all the migration objects within the project and their status as shown in Figure 3.4.E.

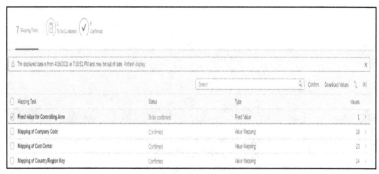

Figure 3.4.E: Object mapping details.

3. Job Management: By default, the migration project is set to run 8 background jobs. Jobs are equally spread between migration objects. We can change this number under job management.

4. Settings: This allows you to change the project settings, including adding additional objects for migration within the project. You can access the SAP object documentation from the Settings menu for the objects within the project as shown in Figure 3.4.F.

Figure 3.4.F: Object details.

5. Finish Project: When all the migration tasks are complete, you can set the project to finished status. Once you have set the project to Finish status, you can also set the data retention period. By default, the retention period is set to off, which means that the project data and all related information is stored indefinitely.

6. Migration Object: Under this column, you will see a list of all the objects that are being migrated within the current project.

By clicking on the individual objects, you get into the object detail screen.

7. Data: Under the data column, we see two pieces of information.

   a. Tables: This displays the number of staging tables created for that object. By clicking on the number, we can see the table name, technical ID of the table, and table status.

   b. Instances: This displays the number of records that have been passed into the staging tables for that object.

8. Mapping Tasks: This displays count of the open and completed mapping tasks for the object.

9. Simulation: Under this column, you will see the count of successful and errored records that have been simulated for the object. The errored records need to be corrected before proceeding to the next step.

10. Migration: Under this column, you will see count a of successful, errored, and not started records for migration.

11. Migration Progress: This column provides a real-time status of the migration once the final step is executed. You will be able to see the number of records that errored out, successfully loaded and records not yet processed as a percentage.

12. Action: This lists the available actions to be performed in sequence for migration.

    a. Download Template: The migration template can be downloaded under this step.

    b. Upload File: The populated file is uploaded into the system under this step.

c. Prepare: This step prepares the staging tables for the object being migrated.

d. Mapping Tasks: The source of target mappings is completed under in this step.

e. Simulate: The mapped data is simulated to check for errors.

f. Migrate: This is the final step in the migration process where data is transferred into the S/4HANA Cloud system.

g. Create a Correction File: in this step, you can generate a file that contains error records. These records need to be corrected and uploaded back into the system.

Migration Object

The migration object is a data object that is being migrated into SAP S/4HANA Cloud system. The *Data Migration Cockpit* app comes with over 150 objects pre-delivered across different process areas. Users can download templates for these objects and start performing migrations. SAP also provides documentation for each of these objects that can be accessed via the app to review the data and field level requirements.

A few examples of the migration object include the Cost Center, Product, Customer, Supplier, Projects, and GL balances.

Migration Object Screen

The migration object screen, as shown in Figure 3.4.G, it contains the following:

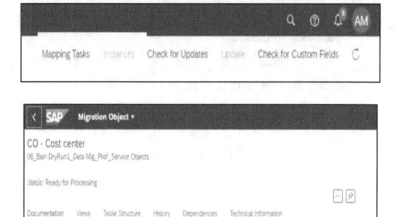

Figure 3.4.G: Object details.

1. Status: Possible options include:
    a. Ready for Processing: Migration activities can be performed under this status.
    b. Not Ready for Processing: Migration activities cannot be performed. This status is usually displayed when (a) the object has just been added into the project, the status is updated to *Ready for Processing* within 1 to 5 minutes subsequently or (b) when SAP is performing updates to the migration object schema.
2. Mapping Tasks: This displays a list of mapping tasks that are required for the selected object, shows the status of each of those tasks, and type of mapping as shown in Figure 3.3H.

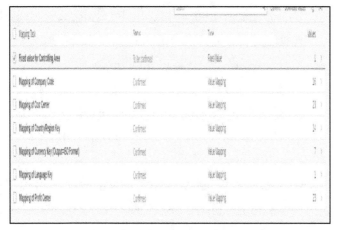

Figure 3.4.H: Object mapping details.

By clicking on a specific mapping task, you can see the values being mapped as shown in Figure 3.4.I.

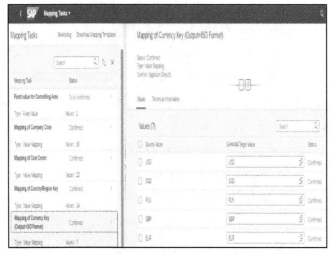

Figure 3.4.I: Object mapping details.

3. Instances: This displays a list of all the records that were uploaded for migration. It lists all the records, including errors, ready to load and successfully loaded. You can filter the results on this screen based on the object type.

4. Check for Updates: When you click this button, SAP checks for updates for a specific object and provides guidance.

5. Update: When you click this button, SAP will perform an update on the object if there is an update for it. While the update is being performed, the object cannot be used for migration and its status is set to *Not Ready for Processing*.

6. Check for Custom Fields: SAP checks if custom fields have been created for the object via the *Custom Fields and Logic* app.

7. Documentation: This provides a link to access SAP documentation on the SAP website for that object.

8. Views: This controls the fields that are visible to the object. By default, *Standard View* is enabled. Using business configuration settings, you can reduce the number of visible fields.

9. Table Structure: This displays the staging tables relevant for the object.

10. History: This displays a log of all the actions performed on the object within the selected project.

11. Dependencies: This displays a list of dependent objects for this object. Example: As shown in Figure 3.4.J object

FI- GL account balance and open/line items are dependent upon the selected Cost Center object.

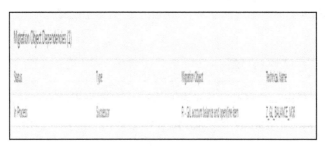

Figure 3.4.J: Object dependency details.

12. Technical Information: This displays the technical ID of the object and can be useful when contacting SAP for assistance with the product.

3.5 SECURITY ROLES

The following business roles need to be assigned to be able to use the data migration app.

» SAP_BR_CONFIG_EXPERT_DATA_MIG
» SAP_BR_BPC_EXPERT

4. MIGRATION OBJECTS FOR FINANCE

4.1 OVERVIEW

In the next few sections, we will review use cases for key finance objects and the step-by-step migration process using the *Data Migration Cockpit* app.

4.2 USE CASE № 1 - PROFIT CENTER

Pre-requisites

>> Company code(s) are configured.
>> Profit center standard hierarchy is set up.
>> Segments are configured.

Migration Steps

Step 1: Access the app *to Migrate Your Data – Migration Cockpit* as shown in Figure 4.2.A.

Figure 4.2.A: Data Migration Cockpit Fiori app.

Step 2: Click on the active migration project to view the details. In this case, we will click on migration for the project **Test Migration Project** as shown in Figure 4.2.B.

Figure 4.2.B: Migration projects screen.

Step 3: Click on **Settings** and **Edit** to add the objects to the migration project. In this case, we will be adding the profit center object.

Step 4: Search for "profit center" in the migration objects search box. The **CO - Profit Center** object is displayed. Select the **use in the project** checkbox to add the object to the migration project as shown in Figure 4.2.C.

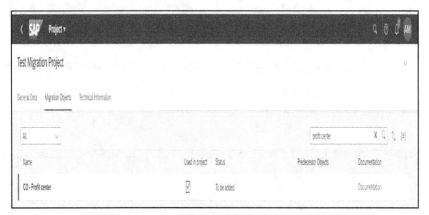

Figure 4.2.C: Migration projects object selection screen.

Step 5: Click **Save** to confirm.

*Note: It may take anywhere between 1 to 5 minutes for the object to be ready for use after Step 5. Until the object is ready, it will be shown under the **Not Ready for Processing** section.*

Step 6: Click to select the CO – Profit Center migration object and click on **Download Template** link as shown in Figure 4.2.D. The template is provided in the XML format and can be opened and edited in Microsoft Excel.

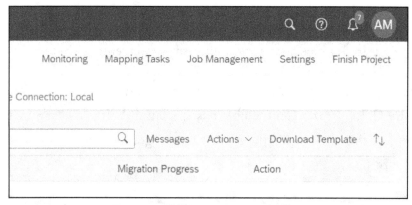

Figure 4.2.D: Migration projects screen.

Note: SAP regularly updates these templates, so it is important that any time you want to upload the data, you select the appropriate object and download the latest template and not reuse the old template.

Step 7: Populate the migration template with your upload values. A few things to keep in mind at this stage are:

» Do not hide, rename, or delete sheets within the template.
» Do not hide, rename, or delete columns within the template.

» Do not change the formatting of the cells or use formulas.
» Review the guidelines provided in the sheet titled **Introduction** within the template.
» Review the **Field List** sheet within the template to familiarize yourself with the required versus optional fields and field lengths to appropriately populate data.

Profit Center Template

The sheet titled **Master record** is mandatory and needs to be populated. Within this sheet, all the columns with asterixis "*" are required, and all other columns are optional. We will now cover all the required and some important fields within this sheet.

Field Name	Type	Length	Notes
Profit Center	Text	80	
Valid - from date	Date		
Valid to date	Date		
Profit Center text	Text	20	
Description	Text	40	
Person Responsible	Text	20	
User Responsible	Text	80	Users need to be set up in the system prior to populating this field.

Profit Center Group	Text	12	
Segment	Text	10	
Lock Indicator	Text	1	Populate with the capital "X" for profit centers that you want to set to locked status.

The sheet titled **Company code assignment** is optional to populate. The purpose of this sheet is to assign the profit centers being uploaded to company codes. We will now cover all the required and some important fields within this sheet.

Field Name	Type	Requirement	Notes
Profit Center	Text	Mandatory	
Valid-from date	Date	Mandatory	
Valid-to date	Date	Mandatory	
Company Code	Text	Mandatory	

Note: *Within the migration template file, tabs in Orange are mandatory and Blue are optional.*

SAP creates the following Staging Tables for the Profit Center migration object:

» S_CEPC for the Profit Center Data
» S_CEPC_BUKRS for the Company Code Assignment

Step 8: Click to select the CO – Profit Center migration object. Then click on the **Upload File** link as shown in Figure 4.2.E under the **Action** menu.

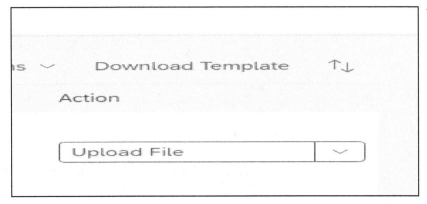

Figure 4.2.E: Migration projects screen.

Once the file is uploaded correctly, you should see a successfully transferred message as shown in Figure 4.2.F.

Figure 4.2.F: Migration object template upload screen.

Step 9: Click to select the CO – Profit Center migration object. Then click on the **Prepare** link as shown in Figure 4.2.G under the **Action** menu. This step is required to prepare the staging tables for the data to be loaded. You can monitor the status of this activity by clicking the **Monitoring** link.

Action

Upload File ⌄

Simulate ⌄
Download Template
Upload File
Prepare

Figure 4.2.G: Migration projects screen.

Note: *Every time new data is being uploaded, the preparation step needs to be performed.*

Step 10: Click to select the CO – Profit Center migration object. Then click on the **Mapping Tasks** link as shown in Figure 4.2.H under the **Action** menu to ensure that all the tasks are confirmed. In this step, we are confirming the values from the upload file as our target values in the system. You can monitor the status of this activity by clicking the **Monitoring** link.

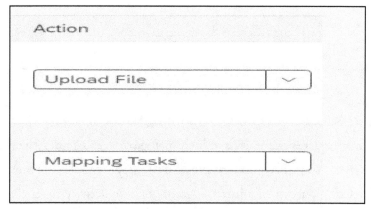

Figure 4.2.H: Migration projects screen.

Step 11: Click to select the CO – Profit Center migration object. Then, click on the **Simulate** link as shown in Figure 4.2.I under the **Action** menu. In this step, the system performs a check for data consistency and displays success or error messages as shown in Figure 4.2.J. You can click on the message number to view the underlying data. You can monitor the status of this activity by clicking the **Monitoring** link.

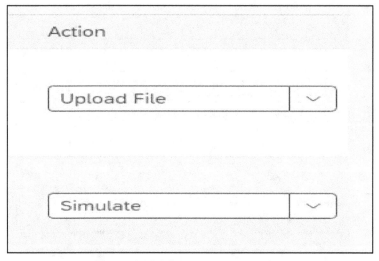

Figure 4.2.I: Migration projects screen.

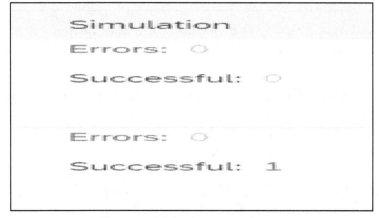

Figure 4.2.J: Migration project screen.

Step 12: We are now in the final stage of the migration activity. Click to select the CO – Profit Center migration object and then click on the **Migrate** link as shown in Figure 4.2.K under the **Action** menu to load the data into the system. You can monitor the status of this activity by clicking the **Monitoring** link.

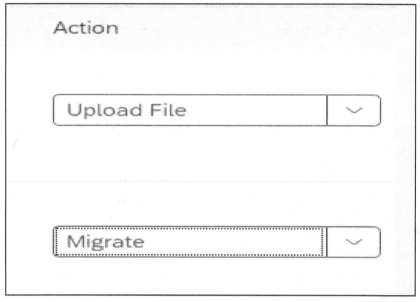

Figure 4.2.K: Migration projects screen.

Note: *Once the data has been loaded, it cannot be undone. In some cases, it cannot be deleted.*

Once this step is completed, you should see a 100% completed message as shown in Figure 4.2.L.

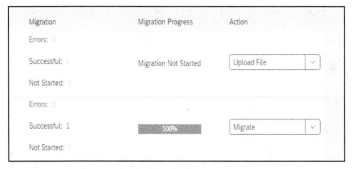

Figure 4.2.L: Migration projects screen.

The uploaded data can now be validated using the app *Manage Profit Centers.*

4.3 USE CASE № 2 - COST CENTER

Pre-requisites

» Profit centers are loaded.

» Functional areas are configured (optional).

Migration Steps

Step 1: Access the app *Migrate Your Data – Migration Cockpit* as shown in Figure 4.3.A.

Figure 4.3.A: Data Migration Cockpit Fiori app.

Step 2: Click on your active migration project to view the details. In this case, we will click on the migration project **Test Migration Project** as shown in Figure 4.3.B.

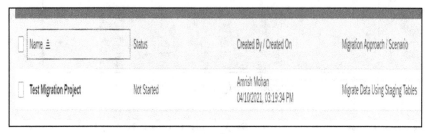

Figure 4.3.B: Migration projects screen.

Step 3: Click on **Settings** and **Edit** to add objects to the migration project. In this case, we will be adding the profit center object.

Step 4: Search for "cost center" in the migration objects search box as shown in Figure X.3. The **CO - Cost Center** object is displayed. Select the **used in project** checkbox to add the object into the migration project as shown in Figure 4.3.C.

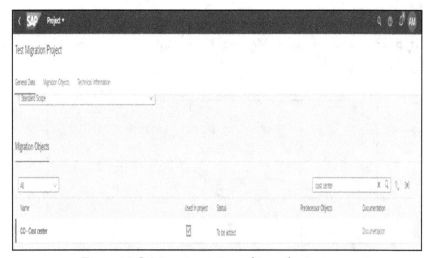

Figure 4.3.C: Migration projects object selection screen.

Step 5: Click **Save** to confirm.

Note: It may take anywhere between 1 to 5 minutes for the object to be ready for use after Step 5. Until the object is ready, it will be shown under **the Not Ready for Processing** *section.*

Step 6: Click to select the CO – Cost Center migration object. Then, click on the **Download Template** link as shown in Figure 4.3.D. The template is provided in the XML format and can be edited in Microsoft Excel.

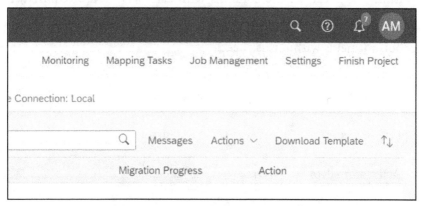

Figure 4.3.D: Migration projects screen.

Note: SAP regularly updates these templates, so it is important that any time you want to upload data, you select the appropriate object and download the latest template, not the old one.

Step 7: Populate the migration template with your upload values. A few things to keep in mind at this stage are:

»   Do not hide, rename, or delete sheets within the template.

»   Do not hide, rename, or delete columns within the template.

» Do not change the formatting of the cells or use formulas.

» Review the guidelines provided in the sheet titled Introduction within the template.

» Review the Field List sheet within the template to familiarize yourself with the required versus optional fields and field lengths to appropriately populate data.

Cost Center Template

The sheet titled **Master record** is mandatory and needs to be populated. Within this sheet, all the columns with asterisks "*" are required; the other columns are optional. We will now cover all the required and other important fields within this sheet.

Field Name	Type	Requirement	Notes
Cost Center	Text	Mandatory	
Valid-from date	Date	Mandatory	
Valid-to date	Date	Mandatory	
Cost Center name	Text	Mandatory	
Description	Text	Optional	
Person Responsible	Text	Mandatory	
User Responsible	Text	Optional	Users need to be set up in the system prior to populating this field.

Cost Center Category	Text	Mandatory	
Hierarchy	Text	Mandatory	
Segment	Text	Mandatory	
Company Code	Text	Mandatory	
Functional Area	Text		
Currency	Text	Mandatory	
Profit Center	Text		
Lock: Actual Primary Costs	Text	Optional	Populate this with a capital "X" for cost centers that you want to set to locked status.

Note: *Within the migration template file, tabs in Orange are mandatory and tabs in Blue are optional.*

SAP creates the following Staging Tables for the Cost Center migration object:

» S_CSKS for Cost Center Data

Step 8: Click to select the CO – Cost Center migration object. Then click on the **Upload File** link as shown in Figure 4.3.E under the **Action** menu.

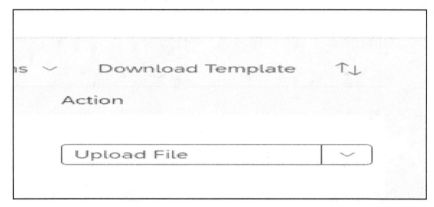

Figure 4.3.E: Migration projects screen.

Once the file has been uploaded correctly, you should see a successfully transferred message as shown in Figure 4.3.F.

Figure 4.E.F: Migration object template upload screen.

Step 9: Click to select the CO – Cost Center migration object. Then, click on the on **Prepare** link as shown in Figure 4.3.G under the **Action** menu. This step is required to prepare the staging tables for the data to be loaded. You can monitor the status of this activity by clicking the **Monitoring** link.

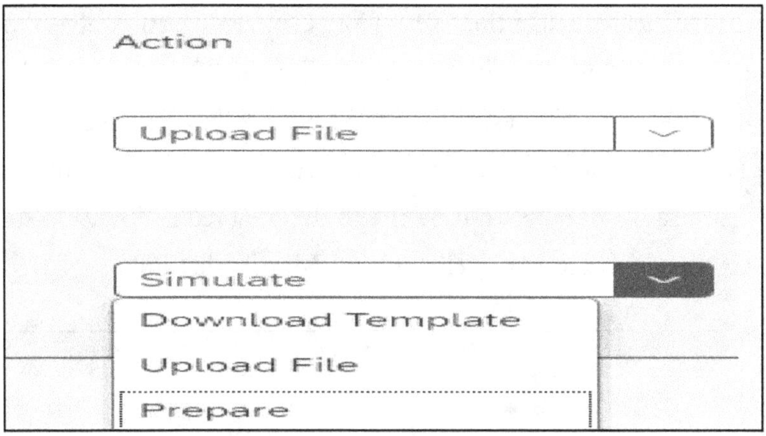

Figure 4.3.G: Migration projects screen.

Note: *Every time new data is being uploaded, the preparation step needs to be performed.*

Step 10: Click to select the CO – Cost Center migration object. Then click on the **Mapping Tasks** link as shown in Figure 4.3.H under the **Action** menu to ensure that all the tasks are confirmed. In this step, we are confirming the values from the upload file as our target values in the system. You can monitor the status of this activity by clicking the **Monitoring** link.

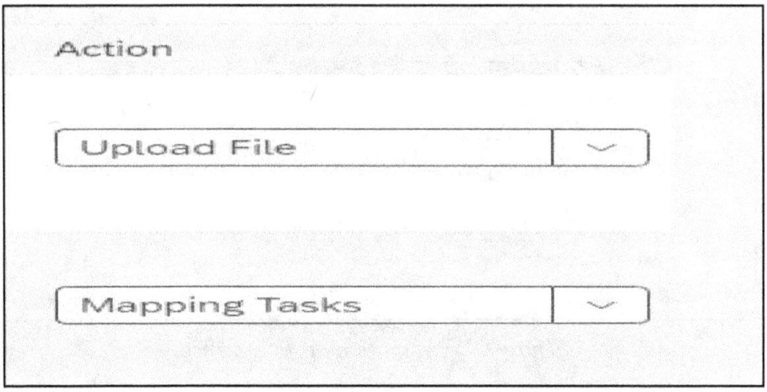

Figure 4.2.H: Migration projects screen.

Step 11: Click to select the CO – Cost Center migration object. Then click on the **Simulate** link as shown in Figure 4.3.I under the **Action** menu. In this step, the system performs a check for data consistency and displays success or error messages as shown in Figure 4.3.J. You can click on the message number to view the underlying data. You can monitor the status of this activity by clicking the **Monitoring** link.

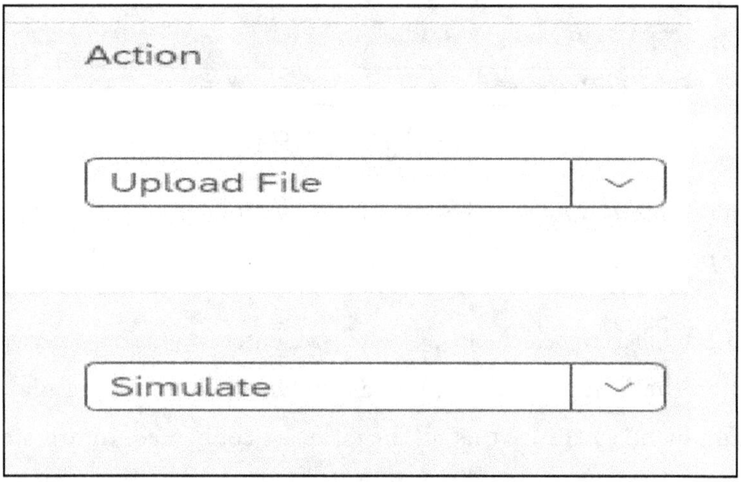

Figure 4.3.I: Migration projects screen.

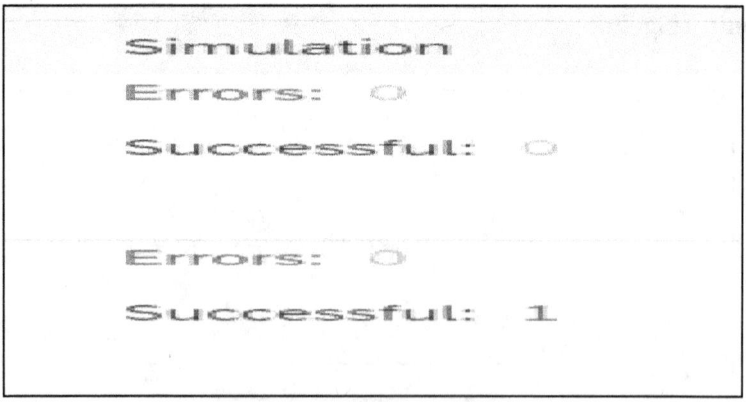

Figure 4.3.J: Migration projects screen.

Step 12: We are at the final stage of the migration activity. Click to select the CO – Cost Center migration object and then click on the Migrate link as shown in Figure X.10 under the Action menu to load the data into the system. You can monitor the status of this activity by clicking the Monitoring link.

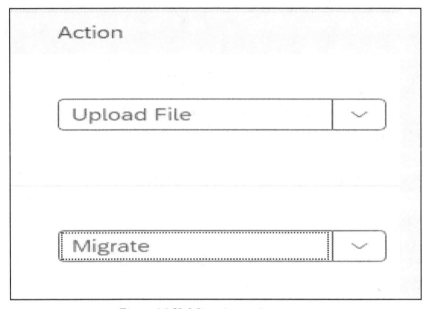

Figure 4.3.K: Migration projects screen.

Note: *Once the data has been loaded, it cannot be undone. In some cases, it cannot be deleted.*

Once this step is completed, you should see a 100% completed message as shown in Figure 4.3.L.

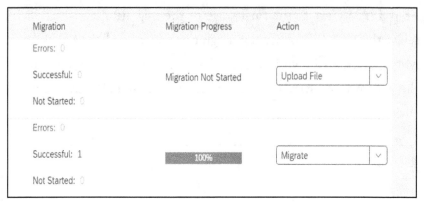

Figure 4.3.L: Migration projects screen.

The uploaded data can now be validated using the app *Manage Cost Centers.*

4.4 USE CASE № 3 – BANKS

Migration Steps

Step 1: Access the app *to Migrate Your Data – Migration Cockpit* as shown in Figure 4.4.A.

Figure 4.4.A: Data Migration Cockpit Fiori app.

Step 2: Click on your active migration project to view the details. In this case, we will click on the migration project **Test Migration Project** as shown in Figure 4.4.B.

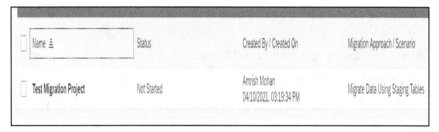

Figure 4.4.B: Migration projects screen.

Step 3: Click on **Settings** and then click on **Edit** to add objects to the migration project. In this case, we will be adding the profit center object.

Step 4: Search for "bank" in the migration objects search box, and the bank object is displayed. Select the **use in the project** checkbox to add the object to the migration project as shown in Figure 4.4.C.

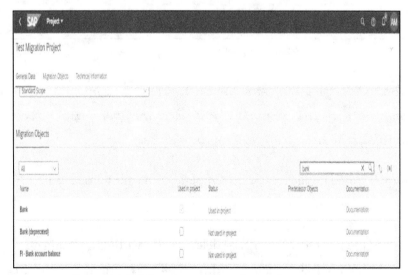

Figure 4.4.C: Migration projects object selection screen.

Step 5: Click **Save** to confirm.

*Note: It may take anywhere between 1 to 5 minutes for the object to be ready for use after Step 5. Until the object is ready, it will be shown under **the Not Ready for Processing** section.*

Step 6: Click to select the Bank migration object. Then, click on the **Download Template** link as shown in Figure 4.4.D The template is provided in XML format and can be opened and edited in Microsoft Excel.

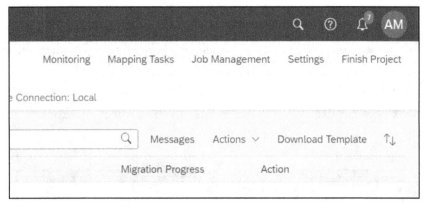

Figure 4.4.D: Migration projects screen.

Note: SAP regularly updates these templates, so it is important that any time you want to upload data, you select the appropriate object and download the latest template, not the old one.

Step 7: Populate the migration template with your upload values. A few things to keep in mind at this stage are:

- » Do not hide, rename, or delete sheets within the template.
- » Do not hide, rename, or delete columns within the template.

» Do not change the formatting of the cells or use formulas.
» Review the guidelines provided in the sheet titled **Introduction** within the template.
» Review the **Field List** sheet within the template to familiarize yourself with the required versus optional fields and field lengths to appropriately populate data.

Bank Template

The sheet titled **Master record** is mandatory and needs to be populated. Within this sheet, all the columns with asterisks "*" are required; the other columns are optional. We will now cover all the required and other important fields within this sheet.

Field Name	Type	Requirement	Notes
Bank Country	Text	Mandatory	
Bank Key	Text	Mandatory	
Name of the bank	Text	Mandatory	
Region	Text	Optional	
SWIFT Code	Text	Optional	
Bank Number	Text	Optional	

Note: *Within the migration template file, tabs in Orange are mandatory and tabs in Blue are optional.*

SAP creates the following Staging Tables for the Bank migration object:

» S_BNKA for Bank Master

Step 8: Click to select the Bank migration object. Then click on the **Upload File** link as shown in Figure 4.4.E under the **Action** menu.

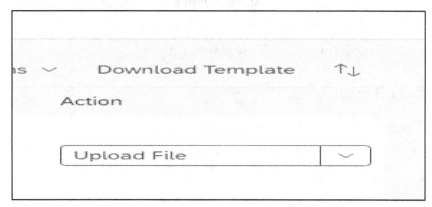

Figure 4.4.E: Migration projects screen.

Once the file is uploaded correctly, you should see a successfully transferred message as shown in Figure 4.4.F.

Figure 4.4.F: Migration object template upload screen.

Step 9: Click to select the Bank migration object. Then, click on the **Prepare** link as shown in Figure 4.4.G under the **Action** menu. This step is required to prepare the staging tables for the data to be loaded. You can monitor the status of this activity by clicking the **Monitoring** link.

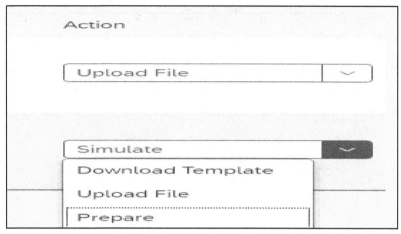

Figure 4.4.G: Migration projects screen.

Note: *Every time new data is being uploaded, the preparation step needs to be performed.*

Step 10: Click to select the Bank migration object. Then, click on the **Mapping Tasks** link as shown in Figure 4.4.H under the **Action** menu to ensure that all the tasks are confirmed. In this step, we are confirming the values from the upload file as our target values in the system. You can monitor the status of this activity by clicking the **Monitoring** link.

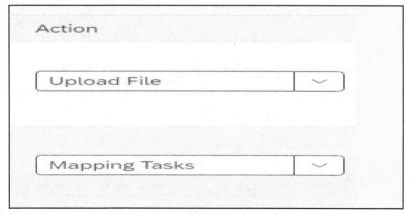

Figure 4.4.H: Migration object template upload screen.

Step 11: Click to select the Bank migration object. Then, click on the **Simulate** link as shown in Figure 4.4.I under the **Action** menu. In this step, the system performs a check for data consistency and displays success or error messages as shown in Figure 4.4.J. You can click on the message number to view the underlying data. You can monitor the status of this activity by clicking the **Monitoring** link.

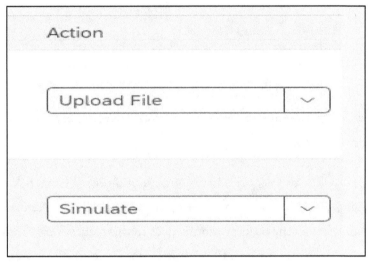

Figure 4.4.I: Migration projects screen.

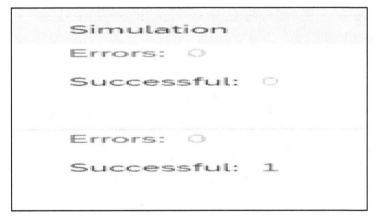

Figure 4.4.J: Migration projects screen.

Step 12: We are now in the final stage of the migration activity. Click to select the Bank migration object. Then click on the Migrate link as shown in Figure 4.4.K under the Action menu to load the data into the system. You can monitor the status of this activity by clicking the Monitoring link.

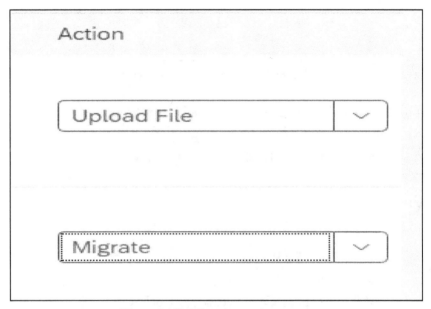

Figure 4.4.K: Migration projects screen.

Note: *Once the data has been loaded, it cannot be undone. In some cases, it cannot be deleted.*

Once this step is completed, you should see a 100% completed message as shown in Figure 4.4.L.

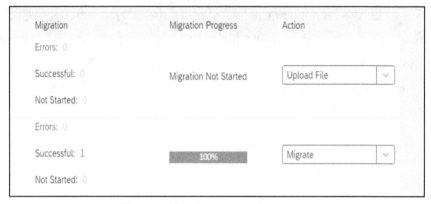

Figure 4.4.L: Migration projects screen.

The uploaded data can now be validated using the app *Manage Banks*.

4.5 USE CASE № 4 – ASSETS

Pre-requisites

> » Asset Classes are configured.
> » Profit Centers are migrated.
> » Cost Centers are migrated.
> » Make Company Code Settings (see below).

Make Company Code Settings

Prior to migrating the Fixed Assets to S/4HANA Cloud, we need to define the Company code settings for the Asset migration. To do this, access the app *Make Company Code Settings* as shown in Figure 4.5.1.

Figure 4.5.1: Make Company Code Settings Fiori app

Here, set the **Legacy Data Transfer Status** to *Ongoing* as shown in Figure 4.5.2. Below is a brief explanation of the three available statuses.

1. In Preparation: S/4HANA system is delivered with this status, and assets cannot be migrated under this status.

2. Ongoing: Assets can be migrated under this status. Once you are ready to perform the Assets migration, you need to set this status prior to starting the migration steps in the Migration Cockpit app.

3. Ongoing (other postings allowed): Assets can be migrated under this status and additional asset postings can be performed.

4. Completed: Once the Asset migration is complete, the status is set to Complete.

Figure 4.5.2: Legacy Data Transfer settings.

Tip: Refer to the link below on **Scope ID J62** for more information on Asset Accounting. https://rapid.sap.com/bp/scopeitems/J62

Migration Steps

Step 1: Access the app *Migrate Your Data – Migration Cockpit* as shown in Figure 4.5.A.

Figure 4.5.A: Data Migration Cockpit Fiori app

Step 2: Click on your active migration project to view the details. In this case, we will click on the migration project **Test Migration Project** as shown in Figure 4.5.B.

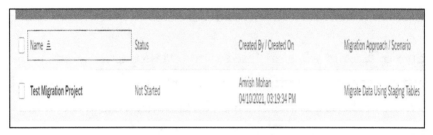

Figure 4.5.B: Migration projects screen.

Step 3: Click on **Settings** and then click on **Edit** to add objects to the migration project. In this case, we will be adding the profit center object.

Step 4: Search for "asset" in the migration objects search box. The **Fixed asset – Master data** object is displayed. Select the **used in project** checkbox to add the object into the migration project as shown in Figure 4.5.C.

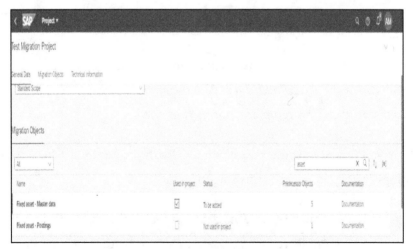

Figure 4.5.C: Migration projects object selection screen.

Step 5: Click **Save** to confirm.

*Note: It may take anywhere between 1 to 5 minutes for the object to be ready for use after Step 5. Until the object is ready, it will be shown under the **Not Ready for Processing** section.*

Step 6: Click to select the Fixed asset – Master data migration object and click on the **Download Template** link as shown in Figure 4.5.D. The template is provided in the XML format and can be edited in Microsoft Excel.

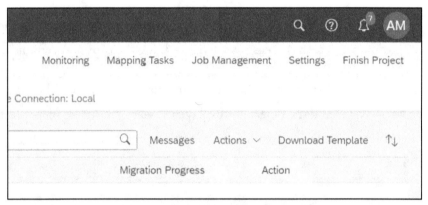

Figure 4.5.D: Migration projects screen.

Note: SAP regularly updates these templates, so it is important that any time you want to upload data, you select the appropriate object and download the latest template, not the old one.

Step 7: Populate the migration template with your upload values. A few things to keep in mind at this stage are:

   » Do not hide, rename, or delete sheets within the template.
   » Do not hide, rename, or delete columns within the template.

» Do not change the formatting of the cells or use formulas.

» Review the guidelines provided in the sheet titled **Introduction** within the template.

» Review the **Field List** sheet within the template to familiarize yourself with the required versus optional fields and field lengths to appropriately populate data.

Fixed Asset Template

The sheet titled **Master record** is mandatory and needs to be populated. Within this sheet, all the columns with asterixis "*" are required; all other columns are optional. We will cover all the required and some important fields within this sheet.

Field Name	Type	Requirement	Notes
Company Code	Text	Mandatory	
Legacy Asset Number	Text	Mandatory	
Legacy Asset Sub-Number	Text	Mandatory	
Asset Class	Text	Mandatory	
Asset Description	Text	Mandatory	
Serial Number	Text	Optional	
Asset Capitalization	Date	Mandatory	

The sheet titled **Company code assignment** is optional to populate. The purpose of this sheet is to assign the profit centers being uploaded to company codes. We will now cover all the required and some important fields within this sheet.

Field Name	Type	Requirement	Notes
Company Code	Text	Mandatory	
Legacy Asset Number	Text	Mandatory	
Legacy Asset Sub-Number	Text	Mandatory	
Cost Center	Text	Optional	

Note: *Within the migration template file, tabs in Orange are mandatory and tabs in Blue are optional.*

SAP creates the following Staging Tables for the Fixed Asset migration object:

- » S_KEY for General Data
- » S_ORIGIN for Origin Data
- » S_INVENTORY for Inventory Data
- » S_ALLOCATIONS for Allocations Data
- » S_ACCOUNTASSIGNMENT for Account Assignment Data
- » S_VALUATION for Valuation Data
- » S_TIMEBASEDVALUATION for Time Based Valuation
- » S_GLO for Local time dependent data
- » S_GLOACCOUNTASSIGNM for Local time dependent data
- » S_GLOTIMEBASEDVAL for Local time dependent data

Step 8: Click to select the Fixed asset – Master data migration object. Then click on the **Upload File** link as shown in Figure 4.5.E under the **Action** menu.

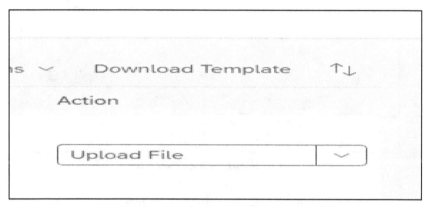

Figure 4.5.E: Migration projects screen.

Once the file is uploaded correctly, you should see a successfully transferred message as shown in Figure 4.5.F.

Figure 4.5.F: Migration object template upload screen.

Step 9: Click to select the Fixed asset – Master data migration object. Then click on the **Prepare** link as shown in Figure 4.5.G under the **Action** menu. This step is required to prepare the staging tables for the data to be loaded. You can monitor the status of this activity by clicking the **Monitoring** link.

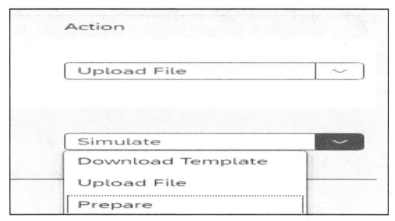

Figure 4.5.G: Migration projects screen.

Note: *Every time new data is being uploaded, the preparation step needs to be performed.*

Step 10: Click to select the Fixed asset – Master data migration object. Then click on the **Mapping Tasks** link as shown in Figure 4.5.H under the **Action** menu to ensure that all the tasks are confirmed. In this step, we are confirming the values from the upload file as our target values in the system. You can monitor the status of this activity by clicking the **Monitoring** link.

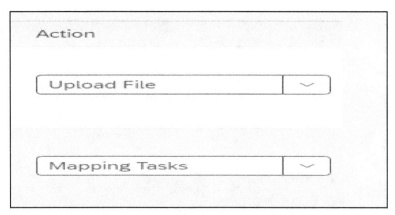

Figure 4.5.H: Migration projects screen.

Step 11: Click to select the Fixed asset – Master data migration object. Then, click on the **Simulate** link as shown in Figure 4.5.I under the **Action** menu. In this step, the system performs a check for data consistency and displays success or error messages as shown in Figure 4.5.J. You can click on the message number to view the underlying data. You can monitor the status of this activity by clicking the **Monitoring** link.

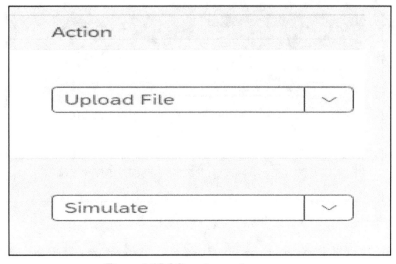

Figure 4.5.I: Migration projects screen.

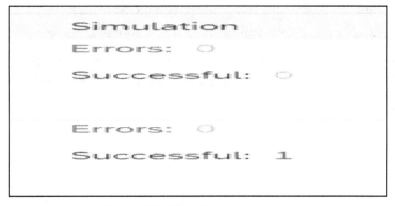

Figure 4.5.J: Migration projects screen.

Step 12: We are now in the final stage of the migration activity. Click to select the Fixed asset – Master data migration object and click on the **Migrate** link as shown in Figure 4.5.K under the **Action** menu to load the data into the system. You can monitor the status of this activity by clicking the **Monitoring** link.

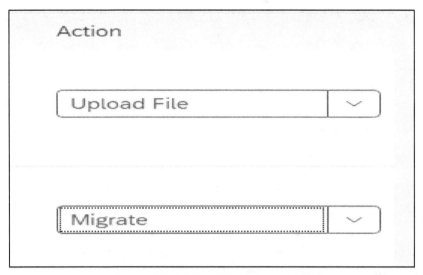

Figure 4.5.K: Migration projects screen.

Note: *Once the data has been loaded, it cannot be undone. In some cases, it cannot be deleted.*

Once this step is completed, you should see the completed message as shown in Figure 4.5.L.

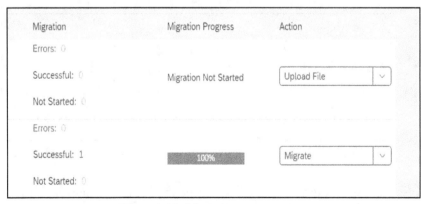

Figure 4.5.L: Migration projects screen.

The uploaded data can now be validated using the app *Manage Legacy Assets.*

4.6 USE CASE № 5 - GL BALANCES

Pre-requisites

> » Profit Centers are migrated.
> » Cost Centers are migrated.
> » General Ledger accounts are configured.
> » Define Legacy Data Transfer (see below).

Define Legacy Data Transfer

Prior to migrating the GL balances to S/4HANA Cloud, we need to define the *Migration Key Date.* To do this, we access the app *Define Settings for Legacy Data Transfer* as shown in Figure 4.6.1

Figure 4.6.1: Define Settings for Legacy Data Transfer Fiori app

Here, set the Migration Key Date to be the balance takeover date and set the Legacy Data Transfer Status to *Ongoing* as shown in Figure 4.6.2. Below is a brief explanation of the three available statuses.

5. In Preparation: S/4HANA system is delivered with this status, balances cannot be migrated under this status.

6. Ongoing: Balances can be migrated under this status. Once you are ready to perform the GL balance migration, you will need to set this status prior to starting the migration steps in the Migration Cockpit app.

7. Completed: Once the GL balance migration is complete and all of the balances have been validated, the status is set to Complete.

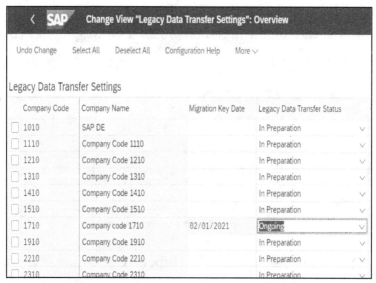

Figure 4.6.2: Define Settings for Legacy Data Transfer Fiori app

Migration Steps

Step 1: Access the app *Migrate Your Data – Migration Cockpit* as shown in Figure 4.6.A.

Figure 4.6.A: Data Migration Cockpit Fiori app.

Step 2: Click on your active migration project to view the details. In this case, we will click on the migration project **Test Migration Project** as shown in Figure 4.6.B.

Figure 4.6.B: Migration projects screen.

Step 3: Click on **Settings** and then click on **Edit** to add objects to the migration project. In this case, we will be adding the GL balance object.

Step 4: Search for "balance" in the migration objects search box, the **FI-G/L account balance and open/line item** object is displayed. Select the **used in project** checkbox to add the object into the migration project as shown in Figure 4.6.C.

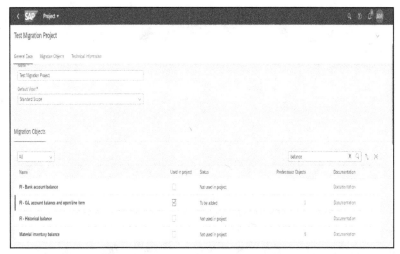

Figure 4.6.C: Migration projects object selection screen.

Step 5: Click **Save** to confirm.

Note: *It may take anywhere between 1 to 5 minutes for the object to be ready for use after Step 5. Until the object is ready, it will be shown under* ***the Not Ready for Processing*** *section.*

Step 6: Click to select the *FI- G/L account balance and open/line item* data migration object. Then click on the **Download Template** link as shown in Figure 4.6.D. The template is provided in the XML format and can be opened and edited in Microsoft Excel.

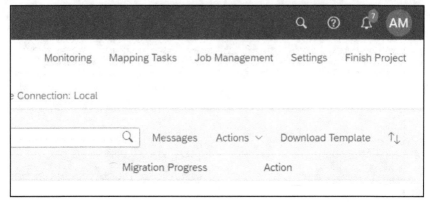

Figure 4.6.D: Migration projects object selection screen.

Note: *SAP regularly updates these templates, so it is important that any time you want to upload data, you select the appropriate object and download the latest template, not the old one.*

Step 7: Populate the migration template with your upload values. A few things to keep in mind at this stage are:

> » Do not hide, rename, or delete sheets within the template.
> » Do not hide, rename, or delete columns within the template.
> » Do not change the formatting of the cells or use formulas.
> » Review the guidelines provided in the sheet titled Introduction within the template.
> » Review the Field List sheet within the template to familiarize yourself with the required versus optional fields and field lengths to appropriately populate the data.

G/L Balance Template

The sheet titled **Master record** is mandatory and needs to be populated. Within this sheet, all the columns with asterixis "*" are required, and all other columns are optional. We will cover all the required and some of the important fields within this sheet.

Field Name	Type	Requirement	Notes
Company Code	Text	Mandatory	
Reference Document Number	Text	Mandatory	
G/L Account	Text	Mandatory	
Offsetting Account	Text	Mandatory	
Document Type	Text	Mandatory	
Document Date	Date	Mandatory	
Header Text	Text	Optional	
Item Text	Text	Optional	
Transaction Currency - Currency	Text	Mandatory	
Transaction Currency – Amount	Number	Mandatory	
Company Code - Currency	Text	Mandatory	
Company Code – Amount	Number	Mandatory	
Group Currency - Currency	Text	Optional	
Group Currency – Amount	Number	Optional	

Company ID of Trading Partner	Text	Optional	
Profit Center	Text	Optional	
Cost Center	Text	Optional	
WBS Element	Text	Optional	

Note: *Within the migration template file, tabs in Orange are mandatory and Blue are optional.*

SAP creates the following Staging Tables for the G/L balance migration object:

- » S_BSIS for G/L Balance
- » S_IT_SPEC for Italy balance requirements
- » S_RU_SPEC for Russia balance requirements
- » S_KR_SPEC for South Korea balance requirements
- » S_MX_SPEC for Mexico balance requirements

Step 8: Click to select the *FI- G/L account balance and open/line item* data migration object. Then, click on the **Upload File** link as shown in Figure 4.6.E under the **Action** menu.

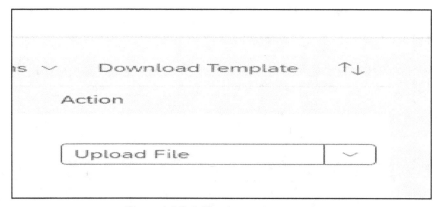

Figure 4.6.E: Migration projects screen.

Once the file is uploaded correctly, you should see a successfully transferred message as shown in Figure 4.6.F.

Figure 4.6.F: Migration object template upload screen.

Step 9: Click to select the *FI- G/L account balance and open/line item* data migration object. Then, click on the **Prepare** link as shown in Figure 4.6.G under the **Action** menu. This step is required to prepare the staging tables for the data to be loaded. You can monitor the status of this activity by clicking the **Monitoring** link.

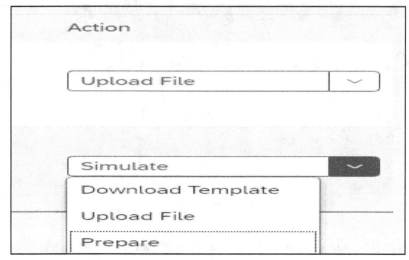

Figure 4.6.G: Migration projects screen.

Note: *Every time new data is being uploaded, the preparation step needs to be performed.*

Step 10: Click to select the *FI- G/L account balance and open/line item* data migration object. Then, click on the **Mapping Tasks** link, as shown in Figure X.7 under the **Action** menu, and ensure all the tasks are confirmed. In this step, we are confirming the values from the upload file as our target values in the system. You can monitor the status of this activity by clicking the **Monitoring** link.

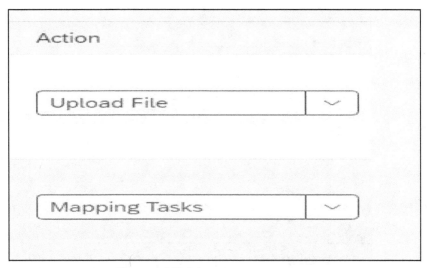

Figure 4.6.H: Migration projects screen.

Step 11: Click to select the *FI- G/L account balance and open/line item* data migration object. Then, click on the **Simulate** link as shown in Figure 4.6.I under the **Action** menu. In this step, the system performs a check for data consistency and displays success or error messages as shown in Figure 4.6.J. You can click on the message number to view the underlying data. You can monitor the status of this activity by clicking the **Monitoring** link.

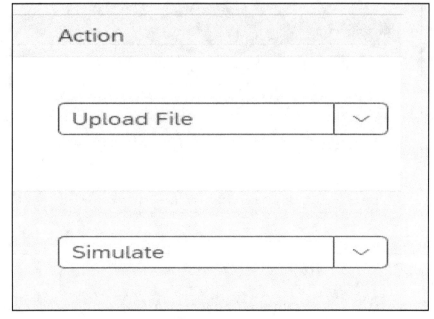

Figure 4.6.I: Migration projects screen.

Simulation
Errors: O
Successful: O

Errors: O
Successful: 1

Figure 4.6.J: Migration projects screen.

Step 12: We are now in the final stage of the migration activity. Click to select the *FI- G/L account balance and open/line item* data migration object. Then, click on the **Migrate** link as shown in Figure 4.6.K under the **Action** menu to load the data into the system. You can monitor the status of this activity by clicking the **Monitoring** link.

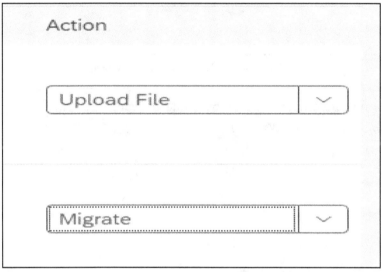

Figure 4.6.K: Migration projects screen.

Note: *Once the data has been loaded, it cannot be undone. In some cases, it cannot be deleted.*

Once this step is completed, you should see a 100% completed message as shown in Figure 4.6.L.

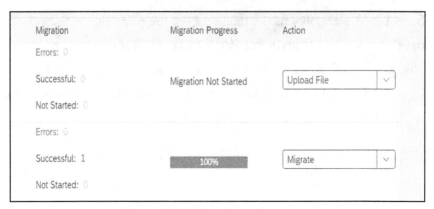

Figure 4.6.L: Migration projects screen.

The uploaded data can now be validated using the app *Display Line Items in General Ledger.*

5. Resources

5.1 BEST PRACTICES

Here are some of the best practices on performing data migrations in S/4HANA Cloud.

» Leverage the Starter/Sandbox Systems – These systems can be used to practice migration in Starter system or Sandbox prior to performing it Quality system. This will help you get comfortable with the S/4HANA Cloud migration process and work with the templates.

» Start Small - Start with smaller loads, preferably with one to four records, and gradually increase the load volume. The main reason for this is that in S/4HANA Cloud, the data records cannot be deleted for most of the objects, so it is important that you do not load data that is not going to be used or is incorrect.

» Migration Projects – Creating Migration Projects for each process area (example: Finance and Sales & Distribution) will help you manage and keep track of migrations more easily. This will also allow multiple users to work on migrations simultaneously.

» Business Teams – Get your business team(s) familiar with the migration templates early in the project. This will significantly reduce your "time to execution". When the business team(s) have the templates and information early, they get the time to source data from legacy systems and provide it in the required format.

» Sequencing – Take time to understand the inter-dependency of the objects being migrated to ensure objects are being migrated in the correct sequence. Example: Profit Centers need to be migrated before cost centers. Cost centers need to be migrated prior to Fixed Assets and GL balances.

» Practice, practice, and more practice.

5.2 ADDITIONAL REFERENCES

» SAP Documentation on data migration process in S/4HANA Cloud: http://help.sap.com/S4_CE_DM

» List of available objects that can be migrated with Data Migration Cockpit in S/4HANA Cloud: http://help.sap.com/S4_CE_MO

» Refer to SAP Note 2538700 for SAP S/4HANA Migration Cockpit object templates.

» Refer to SAP Note 2470789 for FAQ's on SAP S/4HANA Migration Cockpit.

» Refer to SAP Note 2681413 for FAQ's on SAP S/4HANA Migration Status App.

» Refer to SAP Note 2674725 for FAQ's on SAP S/4HANA Migration Status App not available.

6. SUMMARY

For this material, we went over the *Data Migration Cockpit* app and covered the following

- » Features of the Data *Migration Cockpit app*
- » Key Components of the D*ata Migration Cockpit app*
  - » Migration Project
  - » Migration Object

- » Steps for migrating data to S/4HANA Cloud using the *Data Migration Cockpit* app
  - » Creating a Migration Project
  - » Enabling Migration Objects
  - » Downloading Templates
  - » Populating & Uploading Templates
  - » Preparing Staging Tables
  - » Completing Mapping Tasks
  - » Performing a Simulation
  - » Migrating Data

- » Step-by-Step process of converting finance objects for:
  - » Profit Center
  - » Const Center
  - » Banks
  - » Fixed Assets
  - » GL balances

7. ABOUT THE AUTHOR

Amrish Mohan is a Certified Public Accountant and SAP S/4HANA Cloud Finance certified consultant. He has over 14 years of experience in implementing and supporting SAP instances across the US and Europe. Most recently, he has been involved in two S/4HANA Cloud implementations. He lives in Ohio with his wife and daughter. You can contact him at: erp.cpa@protonmail.com.

www.ingramcontent.com/pod-product-compliance
Lightning Source LLC
LaVergne TN
LVHW051536050326
832903LV00033B/4274